ACCURATE SHOOTING IN WAR

By
MAJOR T. S. SMITH
(Late 5th Battalion The South Staffordshire Regiment)

"H." SECTOR, SOUTH STAFFORDSHIRE ZONE
HOME GUARD

(*Winner of H.M. The King's Prize, Bisley*, 1939
and "The Grand Aggregate," Bisley, 1930)

The Naval & Military Press Ltd

Published by

The Naval & Military Press Ltd
Unit 5 Riverside, Brambleside
Bellbrook Industrial Estate
Uckfield, East Sussex
TN22 1QQ England

Tel: +44 (0)1825 749494

www.naval-military-press.com
www.nmarchive.com

*In reprinting in facsimile from the original, any imperfections are inevitably reproduced
and the quality may fall short of modern type and cartographic standards.*

TO

The National Rifle Association and the Small Arms School, in recognition of the very valuable services they have rendered to the Empire, and with hopes that the future may see them working together in one common cause—the encouragement of rifle shooting throughout the King's Dominions.

ACKNOWLEDGMENTS

I am indebted to Colonel Sir P. W. Richardson, Bt., O.B.E., V.D., J.P. (Chairman of the National Rifle Association), to Major-General Sir Alan J. Hunter, K.C.V.O., C.B., C.M.G., D.S.O., M.C. (Secretary of the National Rifle Association), and to Captain E. H. Robinson (winner of H.M. The King's Prize, Bisley, 1923) for reading through these notes and for making many valuable suggestions, all of which have been incorporated.

CONTENTS

	PAGE
EXTRACT FROM WESTERN COMMAND HOME GUARD ORDERS, WEDNESDAY, 27TH AUGUST, 1941	6
PRELIMINARY REMARKS	7
THE ELEMENTS OF SHOOTING ...	7
THE EXPERT	8
THE MARKSMAN	8
GROUPING	9
ZERO	13
PREPARATION OF THE BARREL AND CHAMBER	14
WHEN TO SHOOT AND AT WHAT DISTANCE ...	15
THE HOLD	15
FIRING POSITIONS	17
THE BAYONET ...	20
HOW TO AIM	20
AIMING	21
TRIGGER PRESSING	23
FOLLOW THROUGH	23
IMMEDIATELY AFTER FIRING ...	23
WIND	24
RAIN	24
SAFETY PRECAUTIONS ...	24
CLEANING AFTER FIRING	24
CLEANING GENERALLY	25
OIL	25
MUSCLE EXERCISES FOR CORRECT HOLDING OF A RIFLE ...	26
AIDS TO SHOOTING AND INSTRUCTION	32
ON THE OPEN RANGE ...	36
THE BUTTS	38

LIST OF PLATES

PLATE		PAGE
I, II, III	THE LYING POSITION	16
IV	THE SITTING POSITION ...	18
V	KNEELING	18
VI, VII	TRIGGER CONTROL	22
VIII	MUSCLE EXERCISES	26
IX, X	,, ,,	... 27
XI	,, ,,	28
XII	,, ,,	29
XIII	,, ,,	30
XIV	USE OF SLING	32
XV, XVI, XVII	,, ,, ,,	33

LIST OF DIAGRAMS

	PAGE
GROUPING ...	10, 11
GROUPING GAUGE	... 10
RIFLE ZERO TARGETS, 25 YARDS RANGE	12, 14
HOW TO AIM ...	20
AIM CORRECTORS ...	... 34
THE "LE GRET" AIM TEACHER	35
MARKING IN THE BUTTS	... 39

Extract from

WESTERN COMMAND HOME GUARD ORDERS

Wednesday, 27th August, 1941

1470. SUPERIORITY IN BATTLE.

A German field officer's report that was recently captured by us in Africa said that the Australians were superior to the Germans in the following respects: in the use of small arms, especially as snipers; in making the most of the terrain; in the use of camouflage; in ability to observe carefully and draw sound deductions; in the use of ruses of all types, and in trench digging, which last, the report says, is 60 per cent. of the work of infantrymen.

The report praised the accuracy of fire of Australian snipers, adding that many N.C.Os. had been shot through the head the moment they looked over the parapet, and complained that the Australians were much too cunning for the " simple-minded Germans "!

These are just the things in which the Home Guard can and ought to show its superiority. In its ranks are many excellent shots. There is no reason why it should not know from a worm's-eye point of view every inch of the country over which it may operate. It can test its concealment by looking from every likely enemy viewpoint. Knowledge of the country helps observation and deduction. The Home Guard has many members who combine fertile imaginations with the practical and theoretical knowledge necessary for thinking out effective ruses; and, finally, it has the opportunity now of digging not only primary but also alternative and dummy weapon sites.

But if, like the Australians, it is to prove superior to the Germans who invade this island, the Home Guard must practise hard and intelligently now all the things it may have to do when they come.

C.R.5/4444/G. (T).

J. A. C. Whitaker, *Brigadier*,

General Staff.

PRELIMINARY REMARKS

The following notes have been compiled from the many lectures which I have given to members of the Home Guard all over the country since their formation, and are the result of practical experience extending over a period of over thirty-two consecutive years of rifle shooting, including the four years of the last Great War, 1914-18.

They are not intended to replace any of the instructions given in S.A.T., Vol. I, or other Government training leaflets, but they will, I think, be of some little help to those who desire to become master of the weapon with which they are armed.

One of the main duties of every infantryman is to be able to stalk an enemy machine-gun post without being seen, and then to pick off the individual members of that gun's team.

To do this, skill in shooting is essential, and it should be the aim of every man to train himself to such a pitch that he can guarantee to hit an object at 100 yards and 200 yards, and to go on hitting it, nine times out of ten.

The expert will want to go several stages farther, and the particular part of the object to be hit will be his endeavour.

These notes are not for experts, but for recruits and those comparatively new to rifle shooting.

It is to be hoped that from now onwards and for the next 100 years every boy will be compelled to learn to shoot with a rifle, and that we may become a nation of marksmen just as almost every other country in the world is rifle-minded.

THE ELEMENTS OF SHOOTING

It must always be remembered that no rifle, gun or firearm yet made will put all its bullets, shells or projectiles through the same hole.

All shooting is based on grouping, and just as a hose-pipe will throw a jet of water which expands in size the farther it gets away from the nozzle, so all rifles, guns and firearms will throw their projectiles in an ever-widening stream the farther the range they are fired at. A group, therefore, is a pattern of holes made on a target by a series of shots fired from the same gun or rifle, and with the same aim for each shot. An expert rifleman's ambition is to find the perfect rifle (which he never will do), and so he struggles to get hold of a weapon that will give a smaller group at 100 yards than he has previously known.

So long as the above facts are fully realized and appreciated, we can proceed towards those things which are necessary to achieve a definite degree of skill in rifle shooting.

THE EXPERT

It is not my intention to try to explain how to become an expert shot. To become an expert requires a combination of factors, all of which would require a great deal of explanation, and these notes are not intended to teach would-be experts. It suffices to say that concentration, experience, practice and luck alone are the deciding factors necessary to become a " Bisley champion."

THE MARKSMAN

It should be the aim of every soldier to stalk his enemy, to get as close to him as possible without being seen, and then to pick him off with the first shot fired. If that enemy happens to be a machine gun, then it should be the aim of every soldier to pick off each individual member of the gun's crew with the minimum number of shots fired.

With this in mind, I would suggest that the common or garden bucket be adopted as the standard target or object to be aimed at. It is, after all, about the size of any enemy to be shot at and hit.

GROUPING

At 100 yards a group of 4 inches, and not more, should and must be attained if one is to hit a bucket at 200 yards. A 4-inch group at 100 yards means an 8-inch group at 200 yards and a 20-inch group at 500 yards.

Until a 4-inch group is attained at 100 yards it is just so much waste of ammunition for any shooting to be carried out at longer ranges, and it is far worse than a waste of ammunition to introduce anything approaching rapid fire or snapshooting. These remarks are, of course, made on the assumption that (1) the rifle is capable of a 4-inch group at 100 yards, and (2) the man's eyesight is good enough. Failing (1) the answer is in the hands of an expert armourer, and failing (2) it is useless to persevere until the individual is examined by a specialist and fitted with correct and tested glasses.

Every grouping practice at 100 yards, especially when recruits are firing for the first time, should be conducted over cover (*i.e.*, sandbags), and the forearm, wrist and back of the hand only should rest against the cover. Every help possible should be given to a recruit, and it is essential that he be allowed to get into a comfortable position before firing the first shot.

The leaf of the backsight (P.'14 or P.'17 rifles) should be raised and the slide set at 200 yards.

With the S.M.L.E. rifle the slide should be set at 200 yards.

After grouping, every man should be taken up to the butts and allowed to see his own group, and to have it fully explained to him—size of group, also distance and direction from mean of group to point of aim.

If this is not done, the whole object of the practice and the ammunition will be wasted.

The diagrams on the next two pages show the four classified groups in small-arms training with a rifle.

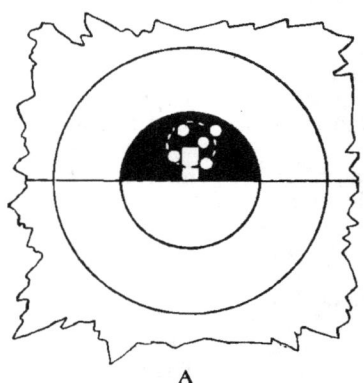

A
4-in. Group counting 25 points.

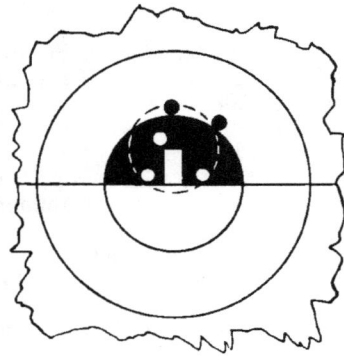

B
8-in. Group counting 20 points.

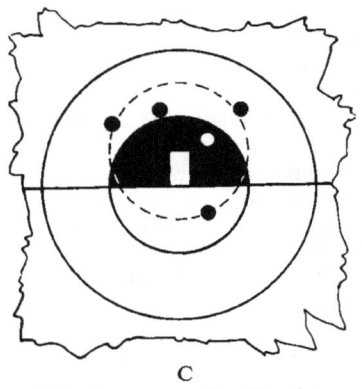

C
12-in. Group counting 15 points.

GROUP GAUGE.

100 Yards.—4-in., 8-in., 12-in. rings.
25 Yards.—1-in., 2-in., 3-in. rings.

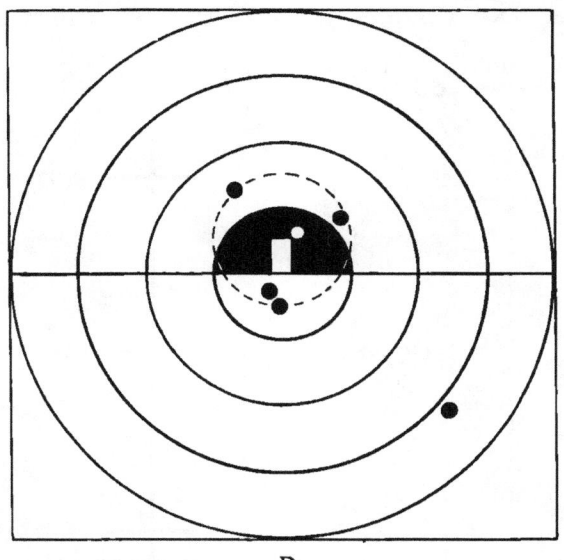

D

12-in. and 1 wide shot counting 10 points (*i.e.*, 4 out of 5 shots in 12-in. group, 1 shot outside 12-in. circle either on or off the target.)

The diagrams A to D are 1/16th full size and show a small 4-foot classification target with a 3-inch by 2-inch white aiming mark pasted in centre of tin hat to give a better defined aiming mark at 100 yards range, the best range for grouping.

The dotted lines show the superimposition of the rings of the grouping gauge. N.B.—Shots that cut a grouping ring count in that group (see C).

Note.—The M.P.I., *i.e.*, the centre of each group shown in the diagrams A to D, is 3 inches above the point of aim where it should be for a correctly sighted rifle fired at 100 yards.

RIFLE ZERO TARGETS, 25 YARDS RANGE, ACTUAL SIZE

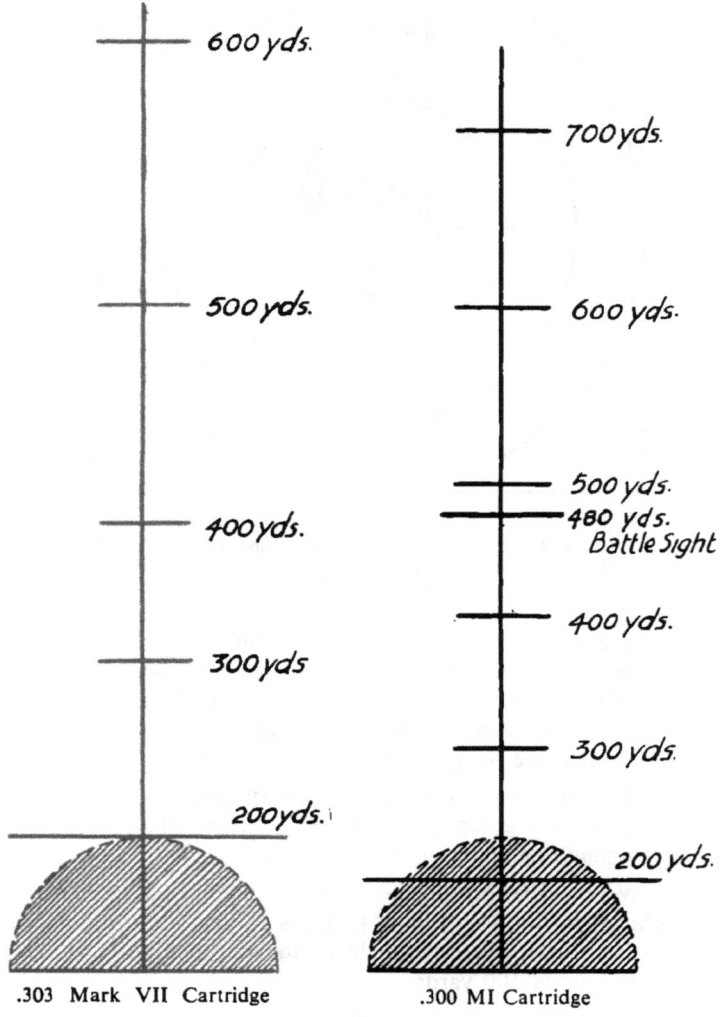

ZERO

One of the first things to be done with every rifle is to zero it. A zeroed rifle is one that will hit an object within an inch or two of the point of aim at 100 yards, and fired by a man who is known to be a good shot.

The procedure for zeroing any rifle for ranges up to 600 yards is quite simple, and the following method should be carried out:—

(1) An oblong target (white), about 12 inches by 5 inches, with an aiming mark (approximately 1 inch)—square or tin-hat pattern—towards the bottom of the target.

(2) A vertical black line should be drawn from the centre of the aiming mark to the top end of the target.

(3) The target should be placed 25 to 30 yards from the firing-point, and plumbed for correctness of the vertical line.

(4) The rifle to be zeroed should be fired over cover (sandbag) with the forearm (not the rifle) resting on the cover.

(5) Three rounds should be fired with a dead 6.0 aim, and the mean of the three shots taken as the centre of the group.

If the group is approximately $\frac{3}{4}$ inch above the point of aim and dead on the line, the rifle can be said to be zeroed correctly for 200 yards.

If the group of shots is either left or right of the vertical line, the foresight must be moved over (with punch and hammer) in the direction of the group, and further shots fired until the centre of the group is on the line. The sight should then be raised to 600 yards and two or three more shots fired. These should also strike the vertical line. If they do not, then the whole backsight is not upright and should be attended to by an armourer.

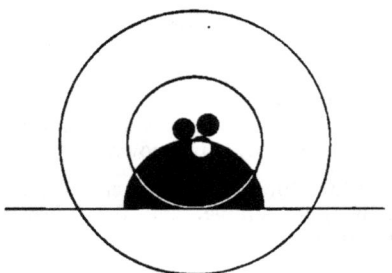

3-Shot group fired from a correctly sighted rifle at 25 yards on a No. 32 target.

Note.—A small tool (foresight cramp) is marketed for moving the foresight either left or right.

If the group is abnormally high (*i.e.*, a minimum of 2 inches above the point of aim), a taller foresight should be fitted to the rifle by an armourer.

If the group is low (*i.e.*, coinciding with the point of aim), the backsight will have to be raised to the 300 yards mark when firing at 200 yards, or a lower foresight fitted.

Note.—A No. 32 " tin hat " 200/25 yards miniature target can be used for the purpose of zeroing any rifle at 25 yards for 200 yards elevation.

THE BARREL AND CHAMBER: Preparation of

No rifle will fire accurately for the first shot unless every trace of oil or grease is removed from the barrel and chamber; furthermore, if any oil is in the barrel, smoke will come from the muzzle and this may give away a position, especially if several rifles are fired at once.

The barrel should be pulled through three or four times with dry flannelette; or, better still, dried out with a cleaning rod and dry patches.

The chamber should be cleared of all grease, etc., by the aid of a breech stick.

Wipe all superfluous oil from the bolt and action, and from the sear and cocking-piece.

Finally, black with smoke any part of the metalwork which may have a tendency to shine.

WHEN TO SHOOT AND AT WHAT DISTANCE

Generally speaking, for all other than expert shots it is a golden rule never to fire at ranges over 200 yards and then only when a definite target offers itself. Opportunities may occur for fire to be opened at longer range (probably at 500 to 600 yards) on groups of parachute troops around their weapon containers. On such occasions, the range should be quickly determined and concentrated fire opened upon the objective by a section of ten or more riflemen. In such circumstances, fire direction and control are essential.

Ammunition should and must be conserved as much as possible, and not a round should be fired unless it is pretty certain to find a billet.

A shot fired prematurely, or at any range over 200 yards, will give your position away to the enemy, apart from wasting ammunition; and the moral effect of accurate fire at the shortest range possible is far greater than filling the air with holes at longer ranges.

It will be seen from the foregoing remarks that, provided no shooting is done at any range over 200 yards, the question of judging distance does not arise and, consequently, will not be dealt with in these notes.

THE HOLD

Many hours of practice in holding are necessary if the rifle is to become what it should be to its firer, *i.e.,* part and parcel of himself.

Whatever position has to be adopted, according to circumstances, every soldier should be able to handle his weapon in the same way as a good golfer handles his clubs, and as a good cricketer handles his bat. It should not require seconds of careful thought to bring the rifle up into the firing position, but should be an almost instantaneous movement.

Farther on, I give some muscle exercises which are invaluable to anyone who aspires to become a good shot.

THE LYING POSITION

PLATE I.—An excellent prone position. *Note.*—Elbows well splayed apart, body flat and hugging ground, making a firm tripod support for rifle—sights upright.

PLATE II.—Butt pressed firmly into the padded portion at the extreme top of the right arm. Right hand gripped well round and as far forward as possible on small of butt. Trigger finger well round trigger. Fore-end bedded right down on palm of left hand—cheek making firm contact with butt and eye well back from cocking-piece.

PLATE III.—Body and heels flat on ground, legs apart. Body 45 degrees to line of fire.

FIRING POSITIONS

The Lying Position

(*a*) Body at an angle of approximately 45 degrees and legs separated with heels flat on ground.

(*b*) Get as low to the ground as possible.

(*c*) Both elbows and chest should form so-called three legs of a tripod on which the rifle rests.

(*d*) Both elbows spread as far out as possible with comfort. It is quite wrong for the left elbow to be directly under the rifle, and equally so for the right elbow to be close to the body.

In the correct lying position, the toe of the butt will be only an inch off the ground.

(*e*) The left hand should be as far forward as possible, with comfort, and should form a cup in which the rifle is rested. It is not necessary to grip the rifle tightly with the left hand.

(*f*) The right hand should grasp the small of the butt firmly with all fingers and the thumb. Remember that it is the right hand that has the most of the work in successful shooting.

(*g*) The butt of the rifle should be pressed firmly into the padded portion of the extreme top of the right arm.

The term " into the shoulder " is a misnomer, for no good shooting can be done if the butt is pressed against the shoulder. Actually, the term " shoulder " was adopted many years ago because a better word for the correct spot could not be found.

(*h*) The cheek should rest on the left-hand side of the butt; the hollow between the two jawbones being the correct spot. In other words, the mouth should be slightly open.

(See Plates I, II and III opposite.)

THE SITTING POSITION
PLATE IV.—Both elbows firmly resting on knees. When possible the heels should be dug firmly into the ground to prevent slipping, if ground permits.

KNEELING
PLATE V.—Kneeling making use of cover. Knee and forearm resting against tree (rifle should not touch tree). Firer sitting well down on right heel, right elbow raised.

The Sitting Position

This position will often present itself and is most useful on downward-sloping ground. In this position, both elbows make contact with both knees respectively.

(See Plate IV opposite.)

The Kneeling Position

(*a*) Sit on right heel.

(*b*) Left elbow resting on left knee.

(*c*) Right arm and elbow out to the side and at right angles to the body.

(See Plate V opposite.)

The Standing Position

(*a*) Turn half-right and separate the legs.

(*b*) Left arm and elbow underneath the rifle.

(*c*) Right arm and elbow out to the side at right angles to the body.

(See Plate IX, page 27.)

Behind Cover

It is always advisable to fire round cover rather than over cover, and one very definite rule must be remembered. Never rest any portion of the rifle against the cover, especially if that cover happens to be brick, stone or wood, or anything hard. The hand or arm *only* should be rested against any cover.

If it is necessary to fire over cover, then let the forearm, wrist and back of the hand rest against it.

As it is highly improbable that shooting on active service will ever permit any of the orthodox positions, it is advisable to practise every other position according to circumstances, but always remembering that the hands and arms will always function in the ways previously shown.

It is also advisable to encourage men to learn to shoot from the left shoulder, as this may stand them in very good stead when having to fire round the left side of any cover.

THE BAYONET

A rifle will not fire accurately with the bayonet fixed, as the added weight at the muzzle tends to upset the balance and natural flip which is caused when a round is fired. It is advisable, therefore, not to attempt to shoot with the bayonet fixed, except at very close quarters.

This does not apply to the No. 4 rifle (recently issued).

HOW TO AIM

The correct aim with open backsight (S.M.L.E.).

The correct aim with aperture sight (P.'14, P.'17 and No. 4 rifle). *Note.*—Foresight and aiming mark only are shown (see text, " Ignore aperture backsight ").

AIMING

With the open sight, as on all S.M.L.E. rifles, the farther the eye is from the backsight the better, and the clearer the definition.

(*a*) Close or partly close the left eye.

(*b*) The blade of the foresight should be seen in the centre of the U of the backsight, and the tip of the blade in line with the shoulders of the U.

(*c*) The aiming mark should then be balanced on the tip of the blade of the foresight (see illustrations).

The longer the sight base (*i.e.*, the distance between foresight and backsight) the more accurate the shooting.

With all rifles having an aperture backsight, the following rules should be carefully followed:—

(*a*) Close or partly close the left eye.

(*b*) Look through (and not at) the aperture. It is not wise, especially with a large aperture as fitted to the P.'14 or P.'17 (American) rifle, to get the right eye too close to the aperture.

(*c*) Once having looked through the aperture and used it, so to speak, as a window, forget about it completely and concentrate on

(*d*) Balancing the aiming mark on the tip of the blade of the foresight (see illustration).

The less you mention the centring of the foresight in the centre of the aperture the better. The lightest portion of any aperture is the centre, and the eye will always follow the lightest portion.

In any case, any slight deviation from the centre will not make any material change in the result of the shot fired.

Note.—If it is found that the left eye is very much stronger than the right, then the firer should immediately concentrate on learning to shoot from the left shoulder.

PLATE VI.—Showing how to grip small of butt with right hand, permitting proper trigger control with trigger finger. *Note.*—Padded portion of the finger between two top joints contacts the trigger.

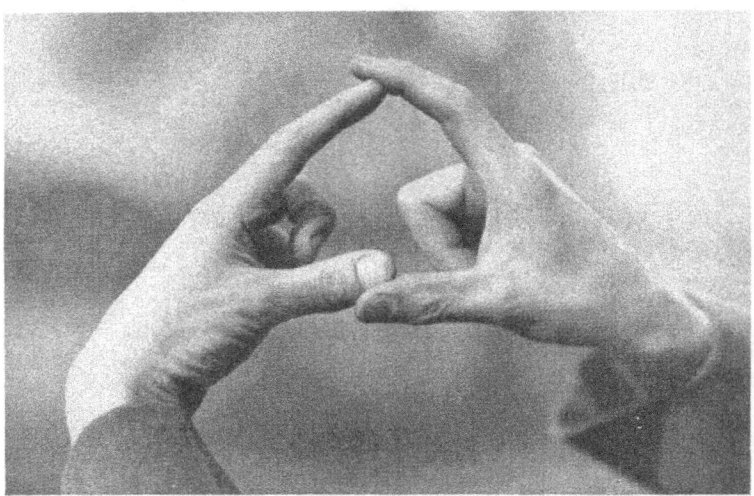

PLATE VII.—Try this for yourself, to demonstrate how pressure by thumb of right hand against thumb of left hand will contract trigger finger of right hand.

TRIGGER PRESSING

This is *the* most important part of all shooting, and too much time and practice cannot be spent on it.

(1) The right forefinger should be as far round the lowest portion of the trigger as size of hand and length of finger will permit. Greater leverage is obtained in this way, and if the padded portion of the finger, between the two joints, contacts the trigger, there is less chance of the smaller nerves, which are in the joints themselves, being affected.

(2) When on aim, *and not before,* the first pressure of the trigger should be carefully taken.

(3) Check your aim again and then steadily squeeze the whole of the right hand, at the same time pressing down on the butt with your thumb until the trigger is released.

Note.—The forefinger and thumb are directly connected and any pressure on the thumb will automatically react on the finger. The illustration shown here will explain how this can be demonstrated.

(4) Breathing should be stopped for a second or two (whilst exhaling) before the final release of the trigger.

(5) Don't anticipate the recoil. Let it take place almost unconsciously.

Constant practice in trigger pressing by snapping at a target is the only way to achieve perfection.

FOLLOW THROUGH

As soon as the rifle has been fired it should still be held to the correct aim for a second or two before coming down off aim. This ensures that the rifle is not moved before the final trigger pressure is taken, and also may enable one to see the strike of the bullet, if visible.

IMMEDIATELY AFTER FIRING

Try to observe the strike of your bullet if at all possible. If it is quite obvious that you have not hit your man, and he has not moved, the chances are that your shot has gone high, in which case aim lower for the next shot.

Do not move about yourself more than is absolutely necessary, and keep your head absolutely still. It is better to indulge in super-slow-motion movements in reloading than in jerky movements. Remember that the words "rapid fire" should never be entertained except when your enemy is in massed formation, and then only provided that supplies of ammunition are plentiful.

WIND

If the foregoing hints have been carefully followed and no shot has been fired at any range over 200 yards, the question of wind allowance will not arise. Wind has very little effect on the bullet up to 200 yards unless it be a gale.

RAIN

Keep your ammunition and breech as dry as possible. The former should not be exposed to the rain, and the latter can be kept dry by closing the bolt as quickly as possible.

The effect of a wet cartridge case is to cause the bullet to strike several inches high.

SAFETY PRECAUTIONS

(a) The safety catch is mainly to prevent the bolt from being opened accidentally, and not to prevent the trigger being pressed.

(b) When moving about with a loaded rifle, it is better to close the bolt on top of the uppermost round in the magazine.

Never keep a round in the chamber with the rifle cocked and safety catch on.

CLEANING AFTER FIRING

One of the simplest and quickest ways of cleaning out after firing is to soak a small piece of four-by-two in cold water and pull it through, several times, on a pull-through. Then dry out with two or three dry patches, and finally oil.

Repeat this for two days at least, and again on the third day following the second cleaning.

Finally, clean out the following week and leave a film of thicker oil or grease in the barrel. A barrel treated in this way will remain in perfect condition and may, if necessary, be put away " on the shelf " for several years.

The bolt, bolt face and action should be carefully cleaned and then lightly oiled.

The " boiling water " method of cleaning after firing consists of pouring a quantity of water, as near boiling-point as possible, through the barrel from breech to muzzle. This causes the steel to expand, the pores to open, and allows the fouling to be washed and cleaned away.

The rifle and barrel must, however, be very carefully cleaned with a dry rag immediately afterwards (particularly the action), and the action and barrel oiled with an oily rag.

Boiling water, funnels and dishes are all required, and as these are very seldom present when wanted I strongly recommend the other method, which is equally effective if carried out properly.

CLEANING GENERALLY

If ball ammunition has not been fired, rifles should be examined and cleaned weekly. The barrel should be pulled through, examined and then regreased; whilst the action and whole of the superficial portion of the rifle should be wiped over with a slightly oily rag.

OIL

If the rifle oil is too thin and too much is used it will tend to fall off the surface of the barrel and drop on to the bolt face. It is advisable, therefore, to stand the rifle, without bolt, and muzzle down, for a few minutes to allow any superfluous oil to drain away.

A light grease is preferable to oil for preserving the barrel.

Important.—The bolt of a rifle (including the P.'17 American rifle) is made for that particular rifle and is not interchangeable with the bolt of any other rifle. Because of this, bolts should never become mixed up. Unless a rifle is kept and cared for by one man, the bolt should never be removed except for cleaning.

MUSCLE EXERCISES FOR CORRECT HOLDING OF A RIFLE

Exercise 1

A squad should be lined up and extended sufficiently to allow the free movement of the arms and rifle.

They should be brought to the standing-load position (*i.e.*, half-right turn, legs separated, and rifle pointing up at an angle of approximately 45 degrees, with the butt resting against the groin of the right hip).

PLATE VIII.—" One."

(*a*) *On the Command " One."*—The rifle should be pushed forward to the fullest extent of both arms; should be parallel to the ground and the correct grip retained by the right hand. Do not move the head.

PLATE IX.—"Two." The correct standing position. Body well balanced on feet slightly apart and at 45 degrees to line of fire. Left elbow well under rifle. Right elbow raised horizontal to ground. Butt firmly in shoulder.

PLATE X.—"Three." The standing-load position. Note eyes on target, heel of butt resting on right groin.

   (*b*) *On the Command " Two."*—Bring the butt back into the shoulder and assume the correct firing position with finger round the trigger. Do not take the first pressure.

   (*c*) *On the Command " Three."*—Assume the standing-load position again.

Repeat the foregoing several times until the muscles of both arms begin to react to the exercise, then stop and assume the rest position (*i.e.*, rifle butt on ground and at ease—muscles relaxed).

PLATE XI.—This exercise is excellent in fitting the muscles of the left arm and wrist to do their job properly.

PLATE XII.—The best exercise for fitting the muscles of the right hand and fingers to take the correct and a firm grip on the small of the butt.

Exercise 2

From the standing-load position assume the firing position (finger round trigger, but no pressure taken).

(a) *On the Command " One."*—Remove the right hand from rifle.

(b) *On the Command " Two."*—Replace it.

(c) *On the Command " Three."*—Remove the left hand from rifle.

(d) *On the Command " Four."*—Replace it.

During these movements the butt of the rifle must be pressed against the shoulder, and cheek resting on the butt—a proper aim being taken.

Repeat these exercises until the muscles of both arms begin to react. Then rest.

PLATE XIII.—An excellent exercise for strengthening muscles of the right forearm and wrist.

Exercise 3

Stand with right foot to the front and holding the rifle with right hand gripping the small of the butt. Extend it to the fullest extent of the right arm until the position is one equivalent to the firing of a revolver.

Do not overdo this exercise, as the strain is fairly great. It will, however, help to strengthen the wrist considerably.

All the foregoing exercises should be carried out daily by all men, and the length of time for each very gradually increased each time.

Exercise 4

Assume the correct firing position and cock the rifle.

A careful aim should now be taken at a miniature target a few yards away, and a coin balanced on the wings of the foresight protector.

The trigger should then be pressed without dislodging or (if possible) without moving the coin in any way.

If all these exercises are practised daily they will do more to help in accurate shooting than anything else.

Exercise 5

Repeat all the foregoing exercises but from the left shoulder—*i.e.*, reverse all movements as if left-handed.

Note.—In street fighting and where fire has to be opened from the left side of cover, it may not always be possible to fire from the right shoulder. Exercise 5 will greatly help to strengthen the muscles of both arms.

Exercise 6

Assume the standing-load position. The squad then close their eyes and the instructor takes up his position at a point about ten yards somewhere in front and claps his hands. Each man will then take aim in the direction of the sound. Open eyes and check aim.

Exercise 7

With gas respirators fixed, practise aiming and snapping at suitable targets in different firing positions. Where Service respirators are issued, they should be worn for at least fifteen minutes during which snapping practice should be indulged in.

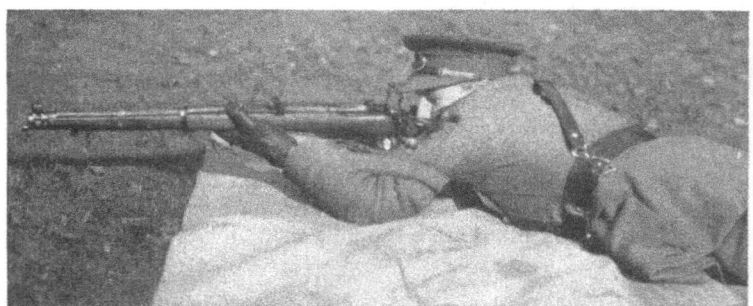

PLATE XIV.—Lying position using sling, one end attached to band, other end attached in front of magazine.

AIDS TO SHOOTING AND INSTRUCTION
The Sling

Every rifle has sling swivel attachments and slings are issued. Besides the question of their use for carrying the rifle they can be used very satisfactorily for steadying the rifle when firing from any position, but to get the best results they should really be fastened, the one end to the middle-band swivel and the other end to a swivel either just in front of or behind the magazine plate.

As, however, it is not always possible to attach the sling except from the middle band to the butt swivel, I will endeavour to show how it can be used in this way.

(1) Slacken off the sling considerably.
(2) Pass the left arm through the sling from left to right.
(3) Now bring the arm and wrist to the left and under the sling.
(4) Move the wrist over the sling from left to right and grip the rifle in the normal way.

When on aim, the sling should be taut and should be regulated accordingly until it is so. Slight tightening or relaxing can be obtained by moving the left hand forwards or backwards.

During the last Great War I fired many thousands of rounds of S.A.A. from all positions, and in practically every case used the sling in this way.

USE OF SLING AS ISSUED AS AN AID TO STEADY HOLDING

PLATE XV.—First pass the left arm through the sling as shown.

PLATE XVI.—Next bend the left arm up and pass the left hand between the sling and fore-end.

PLATE XVII.—The correct way to use the sling as issued. *Note.*—Sling should be slackened off sufficiently so as to provide a loop so that in the firing position it is nicely taut to aid holding, but not so taut as to cause a strained and uncomfortable position.

Clothing

Do not try to shoot in scanty clothing. The more clothes you can wear, within reason, the better, but reduce unnecessary movements to a minimum.

Aim Correctors

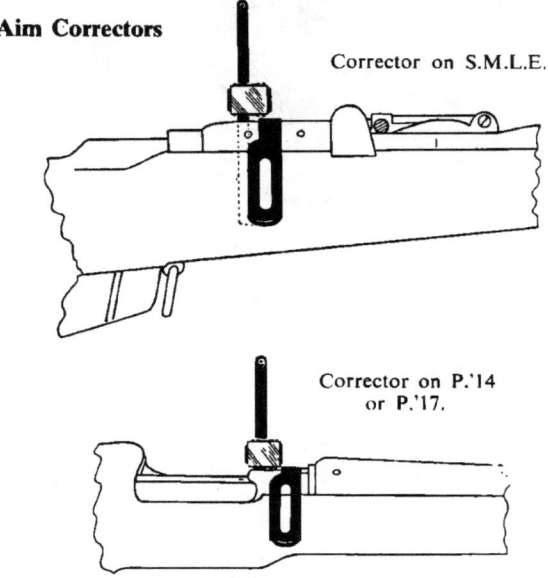

Corrector on S.M.L.E.

Corrector on P.'14 or P.'17.

Aim Corrector

This consists of a metal clip and adapter to hold a piece of plain glass, fixed at an angle of 45 degrees to the line of fire. It was originally made for use with the S.M.L.E. rifle and clipped in a position just behind the backsight. It can, however, be used with the P.'14 or P.'17 rifle, and should be placed in a position just in front of the " knox form."

The instructor lies down on the right-hand side of the firer and looks into the glass, when a view of the foresight and target can be clearly observed and corrected when necessary.

This little instrument is one of the best of all for teaching recruits to shoot.

The "Le Gret" Aim Teacher

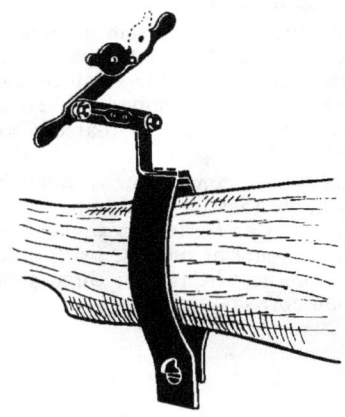

In principle, this is really a movable aperture which can be fastened to the butt of the rifle when in an aiming rest, and can be adjusted so that when a recruit looks through the hole he can see only one thing (*i.e.*, a completely correct aim).

Caution.—One very common fault with all except those *who know* is to be noticed when men get down on to the firing-point, bring their rifles up to fire over or round cover, and when crawling along the ground.

Be particularly careful not to allow any dirt or foreign matter of any kind to enter the muzzle. If it does and a shot is fired the firer may quite well wake up in hospital some hours later.

The Recoil

Quite 75 per cent. of all recruits suffer from "gun shyness" owing to the recoil of the rifle, and this may last for some considerable time before they are cured of it. It is also the cause of 75 per cent. of bad trigger pressing.

Provided that the rifle is held properly, the recoil should hardly be noticed.

It will, however, cause a certain amount of bumping or bruising to the cheek for the first few shoots, and the third finger (wrapped round the small of the butt) may come into contact with the upper lip. To correct this, draw the head back a shade so that the cheek is well away from the right hand.

It may interest and console many sufferers from this complaint to know that in spite of having indulged in rifle shooting for over thirty-two years, and of having achieved a fair amount of success, I still suffer from this same trouble for the first two or three shoots of each season. It soon corrects itself.

ON THE OPEN RANGE

It is advisable not to have more than five details for any one practice. That is to say, if ten targets are available not more than fifty men should be detailed to fire, otherwise there will be an undue waste of time for them and consequent lack of interest once they have fired.

As many efficient instructors as possible should be detailed to help all recruits, and all ammunition should be in the hands of one senior N.C.O. and not issued until the command " Load " has been given.

One N.C.O. should be detailed to the telephone, and he should also attend to the raising and lowering of the red danger flag, when ordered.

The O.C. firing-point is in complete charge of the range during firing practice, and nobody should be allowed to enter or leave the butts without his consent. The red flags, both at the firing-point and butts, must be raised whenever entrance to or exit from the butts is permitted.

Strict discipline must be enforced during all range practices.

Procedure During Grouping Practice

Details 4 and 5 should be sent into the butts as soon as they arrive on the range, and should be under an efficient and senior N.C.O.

Details 1, 2 and 3 are lined up, No. 1 Detail five yards behind the firing-point and a space of five yards between details.

No. 1 Detail should fire on the front row of targets, and No. 2 Detail on the rear targets.

Both details will then be marched up to the butts; Nos. 4 and 5 Details will march out and parade behind No. 3 Detail.

Nos. 3 and 4 Details will then fire in a similar way, and will go up to the butts to relieve Nos. 1 and 2 Details, who will march out and stand easy some distance behind No. 5 Detail.

After No. 5 Detail has fired it will proceed to the butts, relieve No. 3 Detail and will stay in the butts for the next practice at 200 yards (application) with No. 4 Detail.

Correct inspection of all arms must be carried out after each detail has fired.

Application (200 Yards)

Fired without rest or cover.

Sights set at 200 yards and leaf up for P.'14 and P.'17 rifles.

Sights set at 200 yards for S.M.L.E. rifles.

Each shot fired should be carefully marked in the butts and the position of the hole indicated by a spotting disc, if available, or failing that the plain end of the marking pole.

Men should not be allowed to fire at 200 yards until they have made, at least, a 12-inch group at 100 yards.

Nos. 4 and 5 Details, marking in the butts, should be relieved by Nos. 1 and 2 as soon as they have fired.

During these two practices, all recruits should be given as much coaching and assistance as possible.

THE BUTTS

It is essential that all men should learn to mark. It is definitely part of their training as soldiers, and the methods of marking should be carefully explained to them before going to the range.

The Army method of marking is as follows:—

Bull, 4.—Marking disc (white side showing) is placed covering the centre of the aiming mark, and held there for four or five seconds.

Inner, 3.—Marking disc (black side showing) is waved across the target from left to right and back again four or five times.

Magpie, 2.—Marking disc is revolved over centre portion of target for a few seconds, showing alternately black and white.

Outer, 1.—Marking disc raised and lowered vertically from bottom to top of left portion of target four or five times.

Note.—All marking (as above) must be done deliberately and carefully so that no doubt shall exist in the firer's mind as to the value of his shot. Resignal if a mistake is made.

After each shot is marked, its position should be indicated by either the plain end of the pole itself or by the disc, according to visibility.

In the Bisley method of signalling, the value of a shot differs from the Army method, but is very much simpler to manage. It consists of taking the four corners of the target and counting them as follows:—

Bottom Right-hand Corner.—Bull.

Bottom Left-hand Corner.—Inner.

Top Right-hand Corner.—Magpie.

Top Left-hand Corner.—Outer.

The marking disc is placed in the corner corresponding to the value of the shot, and is held there for five or six seconds. The shot-hole is then pointed to with the opposite end of the pole (see illustrations).

MARKING IN THE BUTTS

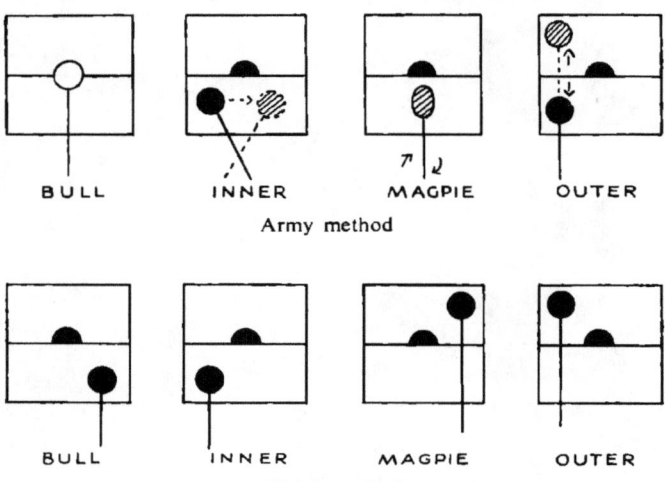

If a shot off the target can be spotted by the marker it should be carefully signalled and its direction indicated by the red-and-white flag.

If in any doubt as to the value of a shot, or whether there is a hit, always pull the whole target down and examine it carefully. This will save endless phone calls from the firing-point and consequent loss of time.

Remember always to give the benefit of any doubt to the firer.

Careless marking and careless supervision will do more harm to the effective teaching of musketry than anything else.

NOTES

www.ingramcontent.com/pod-product-compliance
Lightning Source LLC
Chambersburg PA
CBHW060223050426
42446CB00013B/3155